T0207801

SARAH'S HAIKU

Poems About Living with Hope and Courage

SARAH SHEPHERD

SARAH'S HAIKU
Poems About Living with Hope and Courage

iUniverse books may be ordered through booksellers or by contacting:

iUniverse
1663 Liberty Drive
Bloomington, IN 47403
www.iuniverse.com
1-800-Authors (1-800-288-4677)

ISBN: 978-1-5320-2401-6 (sc)
ISBN: 978-1-5320-2402-3 (e)

Library of Congress Control Number: 2017908025

Print information available on the last page.

iUniverse rev. date: 05/17/2017

Introduction

About thirty-five years ago, I taught English as a second language at the University of Minnesota. While teaching one special class of Japanese English teachers, I heard about haiku. I read a few poems in a book, but I don't remember them.

For a while, I thought a haiku poem dealt with what you saw (line 1) and then what you heard (line 2) and then how you felt (line 3).

In 2014, my brother, Jonathan Kelley, wrote to me about the concept of a three-line haiku poem with five syllables in the first line, seven in the second, and five in the third.

I started writing these poems in May 2016 as a way of distilling issues I often think about, such as coping with type 2 diabetes, missing children who have moved away, evaluating habits and behaviors, managing relationships authentically with respect, and looking realistically at the aging process. I was seeking clarity of thought in preparation for visits with a therapist.

Sarah K. Shepherd
June 2016

1

After this morning,
you're in a different light.
Amazing surprise!

2

Time. Talent. Desire.
Extraordinary event.
Wonderful. He cares.

3

Haunting melody.
Mendelssohn *Song Without Words*.
Opus 53.

4

I miss my old self.
Flexible. Athletic. Trim.
To Pretoria!

5

Big circle of trust.
Surprising relationships.
Ever-changing roles.

6

Logic 101:
When does blood sugar drop fast?
After glipizide.

7

Logic 102:
What makes blood sugar go up?
Sweets. Pasta. Bread. Pie.

8

Leaning on the bar.
Elbow to elbow. Talking.
Easy. Familiar.

9

Trustworthy. Handsome.
Organized and disciplined.
Loving. Generous.

10

Taking glipizide,
blood sugar lows ruled my life.
Constant fear of lows.

11

Never satisfied.
Defective? Just frustrated.
Strong desires unmet.

12

Dark early. Cold wind.
Big blizzard headed this way.
We're ready. Waiting.

13

Cost Park. Pierre's Knob. Bronco.
Daily fireside social hour.
Big, delicious meals.

14

Pause for reflection.
Singular concentration.
Which color to use.

15

Lying on the deck.
Warm sun, salt air, total peace.
Soft waves under me.

16

Caution. Don't grab things.
How should I express anger?
Be advised. Don't grab.

17

Share the same vision,
and everything works smoothly.
We walk together.

18

Deep apology.
Tormented by past mistakes.
Global forgiveness.

19

One bite. The first bite
presents the only challenge.
Resist this and win.

20

The shadow side lurks.
Your self-doubt makes life harder.
Please. Change your focus.

21

Greetings, D and D.
Two names with same first letter.
Instant disaster.

22

Oops. Big bad surprise.
Impossible to change course.
Do the best you can.

23

Mid to late morning.
Calm control or sugar high?
That is the question.

24

Be compliant, please.
You will enjoy the results.
Focus. Hold your course.

25

Mornings are easy.
What changes? Fatigue? Boredom?
Restlessness? No flow.

26

Look around at things.
Each one began as a thought.
Then it became real.

27

Imagination.
Everything begins with this.
Use yours every day.

28

Now say, "I am calm,"
and repeat, "I am peaceful."
Your meditation.

29

My first marriage died.
Unspeakable grief. Huge shock
after forty-one years.

30

It's over. I know.
But love remains forever.
Joys. Sadness. Regrets.

31

"I am calm." (Sounds strong.)
"I want to be calm." (Less strong.)
Always use "I am."

32

An empty spot. Why?
Hmm. What would satisfy it?
Sugar? Sleep? Coffee?

33

My kitchen choices:
Inviting décor throughout.
Warm. Comfortable.

34

At dinner one night,
smiles hid emotional pain.
Facts came much later.

35

Your essence is pure.
Constant. Flawless. Beautiful.
From birth to old age.

36

I'll be the fuckee,
and then you be the fuckor.
Be thus evermore.

37

What is Ritalin?
Is it an amphetamine?
If so, I want it.

38

Advance toward your dreams,
confidently at all times.
Your true self will smile.

39

Bank. Trust. Lawyer. Deed.
Expensive education!
Pay interest and loan.

40

Which do you prefer?
Choose comfort or consciousness.
It's your decision.

41

It's so hard to wait.
Delay gratification?
Try it for a change.

42

Romantic love morphs
to compatibility.
Achievement of love.

43

Different tastes? Yes.
But can you negotiate?
Are you tolerant?

44

Flow zone—a good task.
Below it? Anxiety.
Above it? Boredom.

45

You are what you think.
24-7. Year round.
Best to be mindful.

46

Cheese and bread and fruit.
Major Dickason's coffee.
Way to start the day!

47

Safe. Loved. Protected.
That's how I feel with you, dear.
We're good together.

48

Can't listen. Sorry.
Obsessive rumination
drags me down. Always.

49

Everything she says
reminds me of what I had
and no longer have.

50

Night, Mom. Night, Dearie.
Great way to sign off at night.
Loving thoughts linger.

51

Why am I alive?
To give others life, love, help?
Is that my purpose?

52

Walk. Food. Language. Hair.
Conversation. TV. Joy.
Great outlook on life.

53

Stop what you're doing.
In silence, answers come forth.
One needs time to think.

54

Alone a lot? Yes.
But lonely? No, not really.
I find things to do.

55

What's wrong? Pains? Hunger?
Irritability rules.
Nothing I do helps.

56

I tried this and that,
but no. Each time you found fault.
You are hard to please.

57

Listen to the birds.
The sun warms us on the deck.
Time passes slowly.

58

I want. I don't need.
Big dilemma of the day.
Nix this old habit.

59

Sitting in the sun,
close your eyes. Be anywhere.
Just imagine it.

60

He's asleep at last!
Then five arrived to say hi.
A sleepless night followed.

61

Nutritious friends? Yes!
Toxic people drag me down.
Stay or leave. Your choice.

62

To tell you the truth,
I can't take toxicity.
I need to leave now.

63

Hail to my teacher.
My Mister Steady Eddie.
My loving husband.

64

Outbursts happen. Why?
From fear, illness, or surprise.
Also helplessness.

65

Stop it! I'm leaving.
I'm a positive person.
Can't handle your tone.

66

Show me some respect.
Your sarcasm was hurtful.
Change your tone of voice.

67

What is going on?
Screaming. Swearing. Complaining.
Moody silences.

68

Loyalty and love.
Siblings and children unite.
A lot is unknown.

69

One life is shrinking.
The other life expanding.
How to keep healthy?

70

I will not sit here
if you talk to me like that.
I'm leaving the room.

71

Spending then changing.
What's causing this? I wonder.
Not a good habit.

72

Negativity.
Indifference. Foul language.
Drag my spirits down.

73

Saw it. Nailed it. Great.
First time ever. A new day.
This is real progress.

74

Difficult moment?
Consider alternatives.
Change your behavior.

75

Grow a thicker skin.
Face your pain and deal with it.
Learn how to bounce back.

76

Beware. Some people
enjoy destroying others.
Love—then threats—then fear.

77

The Divine appears
in you and me at all times.
It's a reflection.

78

Clammed up when in pain.
Wish I had spoken. Too bad.
Couldn't find the words.

79

Two types of people:
vibrant and solitary.
Each type has its needs.

80

In the wrong place once.
Unaware of the danger.
Lucky star saved me.

81

Hopus Rex. The best!
Beautiful. Loving Mother.
Colors and perfume.

82

Physically tired.
High psychological stress.
Need a respite break.

83

Big sigh of relief!
Noticed. Noted. Understood.
Sunny, safe home there.

84

Angry? Suck it up!
Your face reflects everything.
Joy or frustration.

85

Resentful. Fuming.
Wish I could be there with friends.
Instead, I hear news.

86

Behold! Or be held?
Thank you! Morning laugh today.
Onward and upward.

87

He was a buffer.
More than I knew. Now he's gone.
The emptiness hurts.

88

Grow old together.
Be easier to live with
as the years go by.

89

Wow! Got it! First time!
Anger that you were deprived?
Or joy? You want more.

90

Curious. No guilt.
Even though you know it's wrong,
but wrong in whose eyes?

91

Calm. The team awaits.
A big plan is in effect.
Stage one has begun.

92

Warm, soft, gifted hands,
sensitive, arthritic, old.
Always responsive.

93

Packed with keys in hand.
Quick kiss goodbye, backward glance.
Heartbreaking to leave.

94

Sadness. Acceptance.
More activities alone.
A gradual trend.

95

Darkened rooms. Long naps.
Hardest part for caregivers.
Dimmed lights. Curtains closed.

96

Shrinking world daily.
Isolation. Memories.
Quietude. More rest.

97

Everything is still.
A blanket of snow outside.
Feel eternity.

98

Designer. Woodsmith.
Gifted hands for love and work.
Always responsive.

99

He held the toy phone
with a sweet, faraway look,
wondering who's there.

100

One simple question
triggers many ideas.
Surprising details!

101

Tremendous appeal.
Energy, focus, and drive.
They excel at work.

102

Behind a complaint
is a longing for something.
Stop. Listen for it.

103

Choose health and wholeness.
Be the real version of you.
Emerge brave and strong.

104

Fun on the playground.
Both give and receive pleasure.
Indoors or outside.

105

Your deepest feelings
and your needs matter to me.
Tell me what they are.

106

Gifted hands nearby.
Caring. Always responsive.
Arthritic. Warm. Soft.

107

Nonvocal. Blank look.
Unable to share feelings.
Anger? Despair? Fear?

108

Which causes more pain?
Words or the silent treatment
or an ice-cold tub?

109

Black spot in brain scan.
This means no activity.
Not now. Not ever.

110

Change your behavior?
Depends on desire to change.
That's the key. Desire.

111

It matters to him.
So let it matter to me.
Then we are a team.

112

Let go of your past.
The best is ahead of you.
Give yourself freedom.

113

Required: after a
sudden unforeseen event,
reinvent yourself.

114

Sharing pain helps heal,
no matter how deep the wound.
You are not alone.

115

I like men who have
energy, focus, and drive,
and excel at work.

116

Increasing fatigue.
His world is shrinking daily.
In a darkened room.

117

New reality.
Acceptance, kindness, sadness.
Caring companions.

118

Inhaling his neck,
overcome by the sweetness.
Every time the same.

119

Warm, responsive hands.
Strong hugs. Contagious laughter.
Dapper. Steady. Strong.

120

All packed. Keys in hand.
Soft kiss bye. Turned at the door.
Heartbreaking glance back.

121

Sad eyes broke my heart.
Headed out. Wept. Stopped the car.
Couldn't do it. Tried.

122

Just stirred in my sleep.
You drifted into my dreams.
Well-remembered hug.

123

Warmth. Talent. Sparkle.
Wide life experiences.
Steady. Creative.

124

Kaleidoscope man.
Complex. Both strong and fragile.
My loving husband.

125

To get good results,
focus and be vigilant.
It will be easy.

126

I know what it's like
to want something you can't have
or what's bad for you.

127

Made my own choices,
even though he disagreed.
He always let me.

128 *(inspired by Mary Oliver)*

A box of darkness
from a loved one is a gift.
Lesson learned: your strength.

129

The senses remain.
Fresh-baked cookies. Gardenias.
Final enjoyments.

130

We'll meet, cook, and laugh
the laughs of a thousand men.
The bond between us!

131 *(inspired by Richard Wright)*

What is the purpose
of meaningless suffering?
To find life's meaning.

132

With whom do you share
your innermost soft, true self?
The sunrise? The stars?

133

Sports in my dotage.
Senior playground always there.
It's between the sheets.

134

Can a person change?
Doubtful. Leopards can't lose spots.
Your nature is fixed.

135

Chased satisfaction
many years without success.
Just found the answer.

136

Morning hot coffee,
mortal life of the body,
tea with you at four.

137

Hard to imagine
eternal life of the soul
from cozy life here.

138

Breakfast in silence.
Alone with my memories.
The new norm, it seems.

139

Walk with me today.
Baby steps. Nice and easy.
Neat and organized.

140

It took sixteen years
to perform at this level.
It's sweet. Effortless.

141

You. Me. This moment.
Body language, tone, or words?
Which one strikes you first?

142

Second spouse a shock.
Totally unlike the first.
Easier this way.

143

Hold it! Stop. Focus.
Barrage of information
can make you crazy.

144

Thoughts on remarriage:
Not as easy as it looks.
Adjust here and there.

145

Organization
and clarity bring comfort.
Life becomes stress-free.

146

Agenda today:
Exercise. Eat well. Steinway.
Play Chopin *Berceuse*.

147

Habits have three points.
First: trigger. Next: behavior.
Last: reward. Good? Bad?

Printed in the United States
By Bookmasters